Jesse Owens

OLYMPIC HERO

Jesse Owens

OLYMPIC HERO

by Francene Sabin
illustrated by Hal Frenck

Troll Associates

Metric Equivalents

100-yard dash = 91 meters

220-yard dash = 200 meters

220-yard low hurdles = 200 meters

1 foot = 30.5 centimeters

1 acre = .4 hectares

Library of Congress Cataloging in Publication Data

Sabin, Francene.
   Jesse Owens, Olympic hero.

     Summary: A brief biography of the black athlete who
won four gold medals in the 1936 Olympics.
     1. Owens, Jesse, 1913-1980—Juvenile literature.
2. Track and field athletes—United States—Biography—
Juvenile literature. [1. Owens, Jesse, 1913-1980.
2. Track and field athletes. 3. Afro-Americans—
Biography] I. Frenck, Hal, ill. II. Title.
GV697.09S23   1986   796.4'2'0924 [B] [92]   85-1101
ISBN 0-8167-0551-8 (lib. bdg.)
ISBN 0-8167-0552-6 (pbk.)

10 9 8 7 6 5 4

Jesse Owens

OLYMPIC HERO

Every morning before school, young Jesse
Owens and his coach met on the high-school
athletic field. For forty-five minutes, the teenager worked out on the track before he had to
hurry off to class. Jesse would have liked to
practice with the rest of the track team in the
afternoon. But he couldn't, because he had to go
to work. The money he earned helped to support
the Owens family.

There were many times when young Jesse Owens felt like skipping those early-morning practices. But Coach Charles Riley never missed one, so the young runner made sure he got there, too. It was worth the effort, Jesse had to admit. He was getting faster and stronger as the weeks went by. Still, he couldn't understand Mr. Riley's reaction when he finished his hundred-yard dash one bright spring morning.

As Jesse flew past the finish line, Coach Riley clicked off his stopwatch. The coach looked at his watch once, looked again, and shook his head. Then he clicked on the watch and held it to his ear, to make sure it was really working. Jesse watched all this, wondering what was wrong.

Mr. Riley took a tape measure out of his pocket, walked to the starting line, and began to measure the distance from start to finish. Now Jesse was even more puzzled, especially when Mr. Riley measured the distance a second time.

"Is something wrong, Coach?" Jesse finally asked.

Mr. Riley came up to the bewildered teenager and put a hand on his shoulder. "Jesse," Mr. Riley said, "you have just done what no other high-school athlete has ever done. You have tied the world record for the hundred-yard dash!"

Jesse was amazed. He knew he could run faster than the other Cleveland, Ohio, high-school students he competed against at track meets. But a world record! Of course, Jesse understood that running a record time in practice would not get into any record book. Yet now that he had done it, he knew he could do it again. Just give him a chance.

When James Cleveland Owens was born, on September 12, 1913, it looked like he would not have a chance even to live for very long. There was certainly no reason to imagine that the child would grow up to be the world's fastest human.

Jesse's first years were spent in Oakville, Alabama, living in poverty. His father and mother, Henry and Emma Owens, were sharecroppers. They lived on a fifty-acre farm. There they grew cotton for Mr. John Clannon, who owned the farm.

Mr. Clannon owned 250 acres of land, which were farmed by eight families of sharecroppers. A sharecropper bought seeds—usually cotton seeds—from the landowner. Then he planted the seeds, raised the crop, and harvested it. When the crop was sold, the landowner and sharecropper shared the profits.

Sharecropping might sound like a fair arrangement, but it rarely was. The sharecropper was forced to buy food, clothing, tools, seed, and every other necessity from the landowner. The owner figured up the amount owed to him at the end of the year. He subtracted that amount from the profit the sharecropper was supposed to receive. It usually worked out that what the sharecropper owed was more than any profit made on the crops. Year by year, most sharecroppers got deeper into debt. It was a kind of poverty from which there was no escape. Sharecroppers who complained about the landowner's bookkeeping were often told to pack up and move.

Like most sharecroppers, Jesse's parents lived in constant fear of angering the landowner. They knew they were being cheated by Mr. Clannon, but there was nothing they could do. They weren't able to read or do arithmetic, which meant they had no way to check Mr. Clannon's numbers and store bills.

14

Yet Mr. and Mrs. Owens were lucky in one way. They had six strong children who could work in the fields. Only scrawny J.C., which was James Cleveland's nickname, was too sickly to help much. His job in the family was just to live, and try to get strong enough to do his share.

Pneumonia hit the little boy every winter. J.C. coughed and ran a fever throughout those winters, but there were no medicines to give him. Also, there were no doctors in Oakville. Even if there had been a doctor, the Owens family could not afford to pay for medical care.

J.C.'s poor health was not improved by the living conditions of the Owens family. They lived in a shack made of cardboard and old wooden planks. Whenever it rained, the roof leaked. In cold weather, icy winds blew right through the house, making it as cold inside as outside.

The only warmth in the house came from the fireplace where Mrs. Owens cooked the meals. The shack had no stove, no running water, no bathroom, and hardly any furniture. On winter nights, Mrs. Owens wrapped J.C. in a blanket and had him sleep next to the fireplace.

Getting enough to eat was another problem. Mrs. Owens had a tiny vegetable garden behind the shack. Potatoes, beans, and corn from the garden made up most of the family's meals. When one of J.C.'s older brothers killed a rabbit, there was meat on the table. The family had to buy all their other food at Mr. Clannon's store. This included the ham the Owens family enjoyed only twice a year—at Easter and Christmas.

When J.C. was six years old, in the winter of 1919, his health worsened. Not only did his pneumonia return, but he also developed a large lump on his left leg. As the weeks passed, the lump grew bigger. The lump hurt him, and made him limp when he walked. Soon, J.C. was hardly able to walk at all, and the hot compresses his mother put on his leg did not help.

Mrs. Owens was afraid the infection would kill her little boy. She sat him down and said, "This is going to hurt, J.C., but your mama has got to do it." Then Mr. Owens and one of J.C.'s brothers held him, while his mother cut into the lump. The pain was fierce, and J.C. fought to keep from crying out.

As he later remembered, "Mama just kept up with what she had to do, and finally the thing was over.... But the 'cutting' turned out to be a real good thing for me...because from that day on, no physical hurt or discomfort made much of an impression on me."

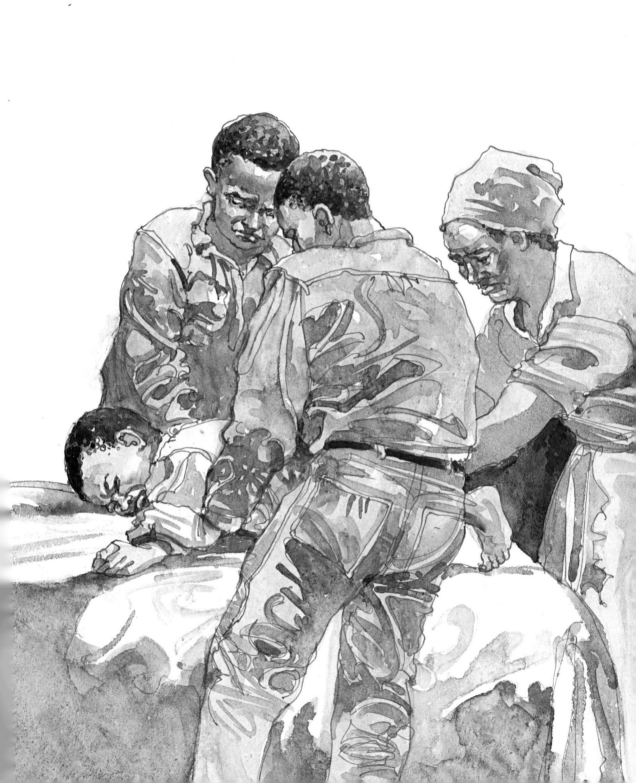

Years later, when Jesse Owens was a world-class runner, he could always overcome pain and exhaustion because of that early experience. No matter how much he hurt, or how tired he felt, nothing could compare with the pain and terror of that operation on his leg.

When the lump on J.C.'s leg disappeared, and winter turned to spring, he was happy. The pneumonia was gone again, and the little boy was able to get outdoors to run around. Running was something special for J.C. That's because his father, whom J.C. loved very much, was faster than anyone else in the county.

On Sundays, after church, neighbors sometimes got together. They sat around, talking or singing gospel songs. In nice weather the men ran races. Mr. Owens won every race he was in, which filled J.C. with great pride. He liked to think of his father as a runner rather than a cotton picker. It seemed a wonderful, free thing to be—a runner. More than anything else in the world, that's what J.C. wanted to be, too.

Running was about the only fun available to J.C. He had no toys or games. There were no other children his age nearby, and his brothers and sisters spent every day working in the fields with mama and papa. And, since there was no school for black children in Oakville, J.C. did not go to school.

For a long time, Mr. and Mrs. Owens had talked about escaping from the life of share-cropping. To get away, they would have to move north, where there might be opportunities for a better life.

But J.C.'s parents were afraid. Oakville was the only home they had ever known. They had never even traveled farther than the small town of Decatur, just a few miles away. They didn't know anyone up north, and were fearful of the unknown world there.

Each time moving was discussed, Mr. and Mrs. Owens decided to stay in Oakville. Then, in February 1921, two things happened to finally change their minds. First, J.C.'s pneumonia was

worse than it had ever been. The eight-year-old boy was spitting blood with every cough. His mother was certain he would not survive another winter.

That same month, Mr. Clannon decided to take a larger share of Mr. Owens' earnings. When Mr. Owens protested that this wasn't fair, Mr. Clannon told him that sharecroppers weren't entitled to more. He had the choice of accepting Mr. Clannon's terms, or getting off the land.

For two days, Mr. Owens barely spoke to anyone. Then on Sunday, after church, he told his family what had happened with Mr. Clannon, and the choice he had made. The family would move north.

After selling their five mules and farm tools, which was all they owned of any value, the Owens family had a small amount of cash. This money paid for their train tickets. It also left them a little to live on until Mr. Owens could find a job.

The family chose Cleveland, Ohio, as their new home. They didn't know anyone in Cleveland, but they had heard that it was a good place to live and work. In the spring of 1921, the Owens family packed their few belongings and took the Louisville and National Railroad north. When they arrived in Cleveland, they rented a small apartment in a three-story, wooden house on the east side of the city.

It was an exciting new world for young J.C. There were sidewalks, paved roads, and so many houses! People seemed to be everywhere. Why, their new apartment even had running water and electricity.

If J.C. walked north from the house, he reached the glistening waters of Lake Erie. There he watched barges, loaded with cargo, headed for distant cities. If he walked east, he came to a beautiful park with wide green areas and a pond where children skipped stones and

sailed toy boats. South and west of J.C.'s house were stores, clanging trolley cars, movie theaters, and lights that lit up the street at night.

Best of all, J.C. started school. He was almost speechless with excitement on his first day at St. Clair's Grammar School. When his teacher asked the shy little boy his name, he whispered, "J.C., Ma'am." The teacher smiled, and said, "Welcome to the class, Jesse." Young J.C. was so nervous, he did not correct the teacher. As a result, his name went onto the school records as Jesse Owens. He liked the sound of it, and he used that name for the rest of his life.

Jesse enjoyed school, learning to read and write and do arithmetic. He also was glad to have so many friends his own age. Jesse's only regret was that he couldn't play with them after school. Even when he was in grammar school, Jesse had to work to support his family.

Life was not as easy in Cleveland as the Owens family had hoped it would be. Mr. Owens had no formal education or skills, so he couldn't get a steady job. That made it necessary for Mrs. Owens and the children to work. On some days, as soon as Jesse finished school, he ran to a local florist shop, where he worked as a delivery boy. On other days, he worked at a gasoline station. He also delivered groceries, shined shoes, and did any other odd jobs he could find in the neighborhood.

Jesse's health was better than it had been in Alabama, though he was still very thin. Despite Jesse's skinniness, there was something about him that caught the eye of Coach Charles Riley— Jesse's speed in schoolyard races during recess. Mr. Riley was the gym teacher at Jesse's school, as well as the track coach at Fairmont Junior High School and at East Technical High School.

In the fall of 1923, Coach Riley asked ten-year-old Jesse if he would like to join the track team. Jesse was thrilled and said, "Yes!" There was

just one problem—the team practiced after
school. Jesse had to work after school. Coach
Riley's solution was for Jesse to work out forty-
five minutes before school. This routine
continued until Jesse went off to college.

At first, Jesse couldn't run very far before he became exhausted. Sometimes he thought of

quitting. He was sure he would never be good enough to win important races. Each time he said this, Mr. Riley told Jesse to be patient. "You're training for four years from next Friday," the coach said with a laugh. That became their joke—the big race was always going to be four years from next Friday.

When Jesse was attending Fairmont Junior High School, he ran in his first interscholastic track meet. The best runners from all the junior high schools in Cleveland would be at that meet, and Jesse was nervous. But his nervousness disappeared the instant the starter's gun sounded, and he won the hundred-yard dash by several yards.

After the race, Mr. Riley told Jesse's mother, "Your son has the most unusual pair of legs on this earth. I know this will shock you, but Jesse could become an Olympic champion." It wasn't until many years later that Jesse's mother told him what the coach had said. By then, Coach Riley's prediction had come true.

While he was still in junior high school, Jesse took an important step toward Olympic glory. He ran the hundred-yard dash in ten seconds, and the time was so remarkable for someone his age that the race was reported in Cleveland newspapers the next day.

The extraordinary runner kept improving. He worked hard with Coach Riley to develop a faster start, a smooth pace, and a blazing finish. As a member of the East Technical High School track team, Jesse was the star in every dash and relay race. In addition, he began running the hurdles.

To race the hurdles, a runner must leap over a series of barriers. These barriers are slightly higher than three feet. Hurdling takes perfect timing in addition to speed, and Jesse quickly became a winner in this event, too.

34

Next, at the suggestion of Coach Riley, Jesse began working on the broad jump. In this event, now called the long jump, a competitor sprints toward a board set in the ground, lands one foot on the board, and leaps forward. The jump ends in a sandy area called the pit. The distance of a jump is measured from the takeoff board to where the jumper lands in the pit. Jesse soon

became an outstanding broad jumper as well as a track star.

By 1933, Jesse Owens' reputation was state-wide. That year, the National Interscholastic Championships Meet was to be held at the University of Chicago, in Illinois. Jesse was on edge. He was going against tough competition, in front of sportswriters and college coaches from all over the country.

What happened at that meet is now track-and-field history. Jesse Owens won the hundred-yard dash in 9.4 seconds, setting a world interscholastic record. He also won the 220-yard dash in 20.7 seconds, and the broad jump, with a leap of 24 feet, 9 and 5/8 inches. In the words of one sportswriter—it was an unprecedented triple.

Jesse was nearing graduation from high school, and scholarship offers were pouring in from colleges throughout America. His parents were delighted at their son's opportunity. No matter how hard life was, they now knew the move to Cleveland had been a success. Jesse Owens would go to college—the first person in their family to do so.

Jesse was eager for higher education and the chance to compete on a college level. But something was troubling him. Time passed, and he did not accept any of the college offers. Coach Riley started to wonder what was wrong, and he asked Jesse the reason for the delay. Jesse said he felt it would be selfish to go away and live well while his parents struggled. Also, the family needed the money he was still earning at his three jobs. Coach Riley told Jesse not to worry.

A week later, Mr. Riley had good news for Jesse. Ohio State University would be glad to have Jesse enroll there. The school did not offer

athletic scholarships. However, school officials
would arrange jobs for Jesse to help him pay for
his room, board, and tuition.

Best of all, O.S.U.'s track coach, Larry
Snyder, found a job for Jesse's father. The job
would be Mr. Owens' permanently, no matter
what Jesse did in college. That was all Jesse
wanted to hear. He couldn't wait to get to Ohio
State.

During his college years, Jesse Owens became known throughout the world. His greatest track performance was at the National Collegiate Track and Field Championships, held at the University of Michigan on May 25, 1935. On that one day, Jesse tied the world record for the hundred-yard dash. He set a new world record for the 220-yard low hurdles, and a new world record for the broad jump. His broad jump was so long that the record leap lasted for twenty-five years.

All this was a preview of Jesse's performance at the 1936 Olympic Games. In those Games, held in Berlin, Germany, Jesse Owens dominated the track-and-field action by winning four gold medals. He took first place in the hundred-meter dash and the two-hundred-meter dash, and ran the final anchor leg for the victorious four-by-one-hundred-meter relay team. Jesse's fourth gold medal was awarded for his broad-jump victory. It was the victory he treasured the most, and he liked to tell why.

In 1936, Germany was ruled by the Nazis, whose leader was the dictator, Adolf Hitler. The Nazis believed that all other people were inferior to them. As the Olympic Games were about to begin, German newspapers called the black members of the American team inferior. This infuriated the ordinarily calm, even-tempered Owens.

The first event in which Jesse Owens competed was the broad jump. He was so upset by the Nazi insults that he had trouble concentrating. To make matters worse, his main rival was a German named Luz Long. Long, a fine athlete, was being praised as a perfect example of German superiority. The competition was being described as a contest that would prove that the Germans were a master race.

It looked as if the Nazis would win their point when Owens made two poor jumps in the qualifying round for the broad-jump finals, while Long did extremely well. Then, as Owens

waited to make his last attempt at qualifying, Luz Long came over to him.

"Hello, Jesse Owens," Long said. "I want to see you make the finals. But you must first relax, and remember something. You do not have to be best in the trials. You need only to qualify." Long went on to advise Owens how to make a safe qualifying jump.

Owens took Long's advice and made a good
jump. He was grateful for Long's help. But
there was something even more important than
the advice about jumping. In front of a crowd

filled with Nazi officials, Long had offered friendship to a black American. This display of courage, humanity, and sportsmanship made a deep impression on Jesse Owens.

Jesse had a chance to return the favor in the finals of the broad jump. After Long made an excellent jump, he limped off to one side, holding a painful leg. Owens hurried over to him. As Nazi officials glared, Owens massaged Long's injured leg to ease the pain.

Jesse Owens won the broad jump with a record leap of 26 feet, 5 and 5/16 inches. It gained him the much-desired gold medal. He also gained a warm friendship that lasted until Luz Long was killed in battle during World War II.

Following the Olympics, Jesse Owens was given a hero's welcome back in the United States. It began with a big parade in his honor in New York City. Everyone respected and admired the great athlete and fine young man. This respect and admiration continued for the rest of his life.

In his later years, Jesse Owens served on youth commissions and as a good-will ambassador for the U.S. State Department. He also remained involved in Olympic activities until he died, on March 30, 1980. The man known as "the world's fastest human" was voted the greatest track performer of the first half of the twentieth century. Although Jesse Owens' records have all been broken, his deeds are a permanent part of sports history!